COPYRIGHT NOTICE

3 Simple Networking Tactics is protected by copyright law. The contents of this book may not be reproduced or transmitted in any form or by any means, electronic or mechanical, including photocopying, recording or by any information storage and retrieval system without written permission from the author, except for the inclusion of brief quotations in a review.

© 2017-2023 by Bart Smith
All Rights Reserved Worldwide
ISBN-13: 978-1544694337
ISBN-10: 1544694334

For more information about *3 Simple Networking Tactics* individual orders, bundled orders, discounts for bulk-quantity purchases, audio products, interviews; information on seminars, JV opportunities, or mentoring/consulting. To book the author to speak at your next seminar, workshop or event contact Bart at:

BARTSMITH.COM

ACKNOWLEDGEMENTS

I'd like to take this opportunity to thank all the people I've ever networked with and those who I can't wait to meet in the near future. To all of you, I say, "It's ... TIME TO NETWORK!"

DEDICATIONS

This book is dedicated to those who might find networking challenging, overwhelming or wish to brush up on their networking skills. Whatever your reasons are to network, I hope these 3 SIMPLE NETWORKING TACTICS will put you on the fast track to networking with success.

WHY I WROTE THIS BOOK

I wrote this book to help anyone who either comes to one of my networking events or others who want to become more successful at networking. Now, if you were to attend one of my networking events feeling uncertain about what to say or do to get the ball rolling, what you need is to pick up this little book and breeze through it in just a few minutes to pick up the precise tactics and conversational strategies that I use to make new contacts, build business alliances and affiliates and make new friends within my industry and other industries as well. Once you absorb the useful content in this book, you too will start saying to yourself, "It's TIME FOR ME TO NETWORK, BART!"

"Hi, my name's _____, what's yours? How did you hear about Bart's networking event? Me too! What do you do? ... That's great. Let me get your information. I'm sure there's a way we can help each other ... Great meeting you!"

TABLE OF CONTENTS

TACTIC #1
MAKE NETWORKING A "MARKETING PRIORITY"

TACTIC #2
IT'S NOT WHAT YOU SAY, IT'S WHAT YOU ASK!

TACTIC #3
BE THE FIRST TO FOLLOW UP & STAY IN TOUCH ALWAYS!

WRAP-UP
ENCOURAGING WORDS FROM THE AUTHOR

ABOUT THE AUTHOR

BART SMITH is the founder of TIME TO NETWORK, a business and personal networking company, whose mission is to help bring people together, network with ease, make new contacts, build new alliances from new partnerships/joint ventures and, above all, have a GREAT TIME in the process! Bart has written other books on networking and enjoys bringing people together.

You can always look forward to networking with Bart and his amazing group of networkers AND enjoying his WORLD FAMOUS CHOCOLATE CHIP COOKIES! You can rest assured that he'll be bringing them! (See BartsCookies.com)

VISIT BART'S WEBSITES:

TVGuest.com
SpeakerCafe.com
TimeToNetwork.com
BreakThroughBS.com
RichCoachBrokeCoach.com
CoachingClientForms.com
ReallyCheapNames.com
ReallyFastBooks.com
BartSmithVoiceover.com
FindTheOneForMe.com
BartsCookbook.com
BartsCookies.com
iLoveBartsCookies.com

... and many more!

BART SMITH
AUTHOR / CHEF / YOUTUBER
BARTSMITH.COM

TACTIC #1

MAKE NETWORKING A "MARKETING" PRIORITY

> "To network or not to network? Is that the question? There is NO question! It's always ... 'TIME TO NETWORK!'"
>
> — *Bart Smith, TheMarketingMan.com & Founder Of TimeToNetwork.com*

BartSmith.com | TimeToNetwork.com | LethalConfidence.com

"MARKETING" IS EVERYTHING!

Isn't it? Without it, how would you find new prospects, new and repeat customers, build new partnerships, alliances, affiliate relationships, meet new vendors, suppliers and those who can either help you with your business or enhance your personal life with new friendships? For me ...

"RELATIONSHIP MARKETING"

... is the best form of marketing! In case you never looked at it closely, no matter what kind of business you're in, PEOPLE are your business, PEOPLE are your market, PEOPLE are the lifeblood of your company, career, income and your lifestyle! Wouldn't you agree?

When you consider other forms of marketing that possess great potential for finding new customers, nothing beats meeting people face-to-face to form new alliances, partnerships, or get fresh ideas on how to do/sell/service something, etc.

They say the average person knows (on average) about 250 people throughout their lifetime. Well, treat that ONE person GREAT, and who knows, perhaps those 250 people can be yours too with just a simple referral. See how easy that works?

What's more, it's not so much WHO THAT PERSON is that you're standing before at a meeting for the first time, it's WHO and WHAT they KNOW that really matters. What do people bring to your table for progress and prosperity? They bring ideas, leads, products/services you can bundle together with yours (for more money/value), even invitations to events/activities you've never heard of before and so much more.

ReallyFastBooks.com | RichCoachBrokeCoach.com | TVGuest.com

Without PEOPLE in our lives, we wouldn't have products to make services to provide, customers to sell to or stores and websites to build to showcase our products/services, let alone people to introduce us to new passions, hobbies and activities. Treat people like gold. They hold the keys to our success, just as we are equally part of their success in all these areas.

"BENEFITS OF NETWORKING"

As if you needed to be told, right? We all have some idea about what those benefits might be. Well, let's nail 'em down and make sure once and for all that we fully understand why we need to **MAKE NETWORKING** a **MARKETING PRIORITY**!

THE TOP 25+1
BENEFITS OF NETWORKING

Here are the TOP 25 BENEFITS OF NETWORKING we should make a PRIORITY in our lives and in our businesses:

1. **Advice** — Got a problem or situation in your personal life and/or business where you need a little advice or a fresh perspective? Ask someone! Surely, there might be someone at the event you're attending that can provide you with their view on what you're struggling with. Share what's going on and see what others have to say in return. This goes both ways, naturally. Maybe you can be that person to help shed light on a new direction or other advice from experience that will help someone else. Sharing your knowledge goes a long way *quickly* when establishing your credibility before you even hand over your contact information or receive theirs.

2. **Brand Promotion/Impact** — Who are you? What do you

do? Tell people and be proud of your accomplishments. Most likely, you're in the business of helping people with a unique service or product. Emphasize all the ways you help people and make their lives and/or businesses better, more profitable, happier, healthier, etc. Bring items that promote your brand, including product, books, press releases, and more to share your brand with ease.

3. **Connections** – This is probably the number one benefit for networking. Who doesn't leave an event without new contacts and connections to fuel their businesses and/or social life? When you make them, nurse them, and treat them like gold. Who knows WHEN these connections will generate their intended benefits. It could be within days, weeks or maybe months or years so be prepared.

4. **Credibility** – What do you know? How can you help people? Asking people how you can be of service is your fastest way to build credibility in the eyes of those you meet. The more you ask, the more you help, and the more credible you become. "Have you met _____? I did, and wow, does he/she know about _____. C'mon, let's go talk to him/her about your situation. I bet he/she can help."

5. **Following/Fans/Tribes** – What better way to grow your network, attract/develop new fans, build a new tribe or feed your current one other than networking (online/offline). Who knows, you might become a fan of someone at the event after hearing what they do or where their passion lies. Take pictures with as many people you possible and post them online. Show people who couldn't make the event who you networked with and help your fans and followers follow those you just met. Reciprocation and helping each other is the secret to everyone making it and succeeding in what we all do.

ReallyFastBooks.com | RichCoachBrokeCoach.com | TVGuest.com

6. **Friendships** — Who doesn't need friends? Did you just move into a new area? Get out and network. EVERYONE there, for the most part, doesn't know anyone either. What a great first place to start building new friendships, connections, get to know your community, etc. "I just moved to town. I don't know where anything is. What's your recommendation for _____?" You'd be surprised how many business owners reach out to invite you to events they're attending in the near future. "I'm having an event next week. Why don't you come?" See how that works? Ask and you shall receive ... *new acquaintances and friendships!*

7. **Fun** — Who doesn't like fun? What's *not* fun is working at home (or at the office) for hours, days, weeks on end without actually coming into contact with other people. Sure networking might focus on business, making connections, helping others and gathering leads, but it's also a lot of fun to dress up and head out to an event. Networking makes BUSINESS MORE FUN! Bored out of your mind with all the work you have to do? Stir things up, get creative, and reignite the passion you have for your own business by heading out and learning about OTHERS. It can be a lot of fun! "I didn't know you also like to _____ (i.e., hobby/interest). We should definitely get together and _____." This doesn't even include what can happen before, during or after a networking event. Some of you might decide to stay at the hotel where the event was held and head to the bar/lounge/restaurant for some drinks, dinner and more conversation.

8. **Get Out & Socialization** — We just mentioned FUN and why networking is actually a FUN event to participate in. It's not all business and work. Getting out of the house/office is always guaranteed to put a smile on your face and can help you build new social networks and friends to do things with. That's a bonus.

BartSmith.com | TimeToNetwork.com | LethalConfidence.com

TACTIC #1 – MAKE NETWORKING A "MARKETING PRIORITY"

9. **Impact** – We all want to have an impact on people (in a good way) and be remembered or at least highly thought of. What better way to impress others than by offering to help them with their needs. "How can I help you? Really? Great! I'd be glad to _____." You can just imagine the other person saying to themselves, "Wow, I'm so grateful I met (YOU) at that event. What he/she said and the help I got is really going to have an impact on my overall success."

10. **Increased Confidence** – There's no better way to increase your self-confidence than by helping others with WHAT you know or WHO you know. Seriously. Confidence comes from three main sources: education, training and faith. When you share those things with others, they add fuel to your own confidence allowing you to comfortably approach other people. Share what you know, what you do, how you've helped others, and have faith in people and recognize their achievements. You're boosting their self-esteem in return. "I believe in what you're doing and think you should press on! You've got my support! Keep me posted on your progress."

11. **Introductions** – How are you going to get introduced to new people if you're at home or at the office? You're not! You gotta get out there, show up, attend and BAM! Watch the introductions happen left and right. You should make the effort to introduce at least three people to people they never met at the event that you did. Also, ask three people to introduce you to people they met that you didn't meet. Just say, "Did you meet anyone interesting tonight? Should I meet them?" Watch people share who they met and take you over to them. How cool! Great way to meet new people, with an introduction!

12. **Leads** – Who couldn't use more leads? It isn't about finding that one lead for your business, it's more about getting leads and contacts from that ONE PERSON who might

turn over their entire database to you, for example. I've seen it happen. "Bart, great meeting you. I'd love to join your affiliate program and share your books and training programs with my list of 25,000." WOW! Remember though, many people are looking for leads. So, help as many people as you can to find leads for their business first. In the process, people will learn what you do and naturally align themselves with what you need and help you. Help others to help yourself. Funny how that works!

13. **Opens New Doors** – Don't you just love it when one door closes and another door opens? That's what it's like when you're sitting in your office wondering why one client closed the door on you and said, "No," to your offer. Then, you went networking and what happened? You met ONE PERSON who said, figuratively, "My door's open for (your) business. Please come in. I could use your help!"

14. **Positive Influence** – Some people you meet might not be as positive, optimistic or high on life and business as you. So? Impact them with your positive attitude, lift their spirits and watch them sing your praises among others they know and meet tonight. Watch them seek you out in the room wanting to introduce you to their best friend who just might be the owner of a company you would love to get to know, but never would have unless you had spread your positive influence with all those you met that night. Keep it up!

15. **Raising Your Profile** – There's nothing better than to be talked about (in a good way) and RECOGNIZED at events you attend. Take pictures and post them on different social media websites/accounts. Show people where you go and network.

16. **Real Time Information Exchange** – Who doesn't have a smart phone, built-in microphone, camera or video recording capabilities? Report to others where you are and what's

going on at the event with photos, texts, and videos. Imagine you're a reporter. Comment on the event and the people you meet. Do this at every event and people will see you as a source of valuable information about an event they couldn't attend.

17. **Real People** – Are you tired of talking to your monitor when meeting new people? You want to reach out and shake their hand, but the screen blocks you from any human contact! Well, not at a live, in-person networking event. Humans are social creatures by nature. Let your social creature out to play every now and then. Attend 1-4 networking events per month just to feel human again! Oh, you'll be helping others do the same in return. A good thing!

18. **Referrals/Increased Business** – Who couldn't use more referrals? Do you have any for those you meet? You better, as in, listen to what other people are looking for (i.e., help, leads, referrals ...) and make note. Keep a list of the people you meet in your head, phone or computer. When you come across people (after) the event who need their help, you know who to refer them to. What a great way for you to poke your head back into their world, when you say, "I've got a lead for you if you're interested." By you looking out for others, you'll soon have people looking out for you. Do onto others (first), as you'd like done on to you, right?

19. **Satisfaction From Helping Others** – It's such a good feeling when you can help other people. Helping lifts you up as you help lift them up. It's just good karma. Maybe not immediately, but in the days, weeks, months and years ahead, helping others usually comes back to you. It's like planting seeds of prosperous times for everyone. So, help all you can. It's going to come back to you.

20. **Shared Knowledge** – What do you know that someone else doesn't know, and vice versa. It makes for interesting

conversation. Never stop learning, growing, or sharing your knowledge. When people see you as a source of wisdom, expertise, and information, watch the leads and referrals fly your way FAST!

21. **Shared Resources** – "Have you ever heard of (resource)? It will help you _____." ("Wow, thanks for that information.") It wouldn't hurt you to prepare a one-sheet list of handy resources that people can tap into if you find that you share common interests with someone. Talk about sending people home with a big *"Thank you for giving me this handy list."* grin on their face after reviewing your list of recommended resources and acting on what they see helps them best.

22. **Source Of Ideas** – Writer's block? Stuck in a rut? Don't know what to do next? Looking for new ideas? Get out of your *rut* zone and head on over to the nearest *networking* zone! There, you'll find new faces with fresh ideas and perspectives on what your next move might be. You don't even have to ask. Just observe, listen and pay attention to what's being said in those circles of conversation that you circulate among. You never know what you might pick up. An idea? New book title? Material for something you could turn into a new stream of income? New product/service idea? An idea for a friend you spoke to earlier who had their own block of some kind? "Hey, I have an idea for you that I picked up at yesterday's networking event. What if you were to _____." When you're cup (brain) is empty, let others fill it for you! GO NETWORKING! It's like fishing when you're hungry for ideas! Head to where the fish (ideas) are!

23. **Strategic Partnerships & Collaboration** – Out of the crowd, you might meet one special person, company or group of people who you might come to rely on for collaboration, think-tank discussions, and the like. You never would have met that new partnership, alliance or affiliate if it wasn't

for networking. GET OUT THERE!

24. **Strengthens Relationships** – Sometimes, you run into the same people at different networking events. When that happens, it's like meeting up with old friends. You can build strong bonds and strengthen those relationships with people you meet at networking events by staying in touch. A good way to do this is by networking often and showing continue interest in their successes. So, again, GET OUT THERE and network!

25. **Support, Encouragement & Acknowledgement** – Who doesn't love a little support, encouragement and getting recognized from time to time? We all do. So? Share what you do and find out what others do and encourage them with their endeavors. Lend support to help others move forward in what they're doing. Acknowledge them for the work they do and what a great product/service they have because it helps people in a wonderful way. What comes around, goes around in the world of networking, just in case you didn't know. I'm sure you knew. So, turn on the support, encouragement and acknowledgement towards others and watch it fly right back in your direction in time.

26. **Widens Your Network** – Networking and attending meetings throughout your local region can really widen your own network of fans, friends, customers, clients and prospects. Just don't attend one networking event, attend several per year, per month, per week on occasion. What's the title of this section? MAKE NETWORKING A MARKETING PRIORITY! That's right! Get out there! Widen your network!

Now, how do all these BENEFITS relate to MARKETING? In one very clear and simple way ... THEY MAKE YOU LOOK GOOD! They spread your name around town. They put your face on social media in ways people wish they could meet you. Networking helps foster word of mouth marketing, excitement, interest and increased energy from people who just met you who now might want to work with you, refer you, promote you, just as you desire to do the same in like return at them. As they say, "What goes around comes around." So, be all those things to people (through your networking efforts), and watch it come right back around to you.

Every one of those benefits can help feed your heart, social life, fun meter, your bottom line, or whatever else you need to gain from networking. Whether its money, exposure, leads, new friends, ____, or? Just name it! Fill in the blank. Networking can do all these things for you and so much more! Soon you will see the value in forming and maintaining a strong contact base that will serve you well for years to come. Simply said, these are the BENEFITS OF NETWORKING and why you should:

MAKE NETWORKING A "MARKETING PRIORITY"

BartSmith.com | TimeToNetwork.com | LethalConfidence.com

TACTIC #1 – MAKE NETWORKING A "MARKETING PRIORITY"

WHERE CAN YOU NETWORK?

Don't know where to find others to network? Here's a hot list that is sure to give you more networking opportunities than your calendar can handle. Be there or *be square!*

Alumni Events	Hobby Clubs	Powwows
Art Societies	Launch Parties	Religious Events
Associations	Leagues	Retreats
Blogging	Lectures	Round Tables
Chamber Of Commerce	MeetUp Groups	Seminars
Classes	Meetings	Signings
Clubs	Museum Societies	Social Media
Coffee Shops	Music Concerts	Speeches & Talks
Conferences	Neighbor Groups	Summits
Councils	Networking Events	Toastmasters
Ethnic Clubs	Online Forums	Trade Shows
Expos	Organizations	Volunteer Work
Gender-Based Clubs	Parties	Where Connectors Are
Gyms	Pet Clubs	Workshops

WHERE TO START?

The first place to really start is your with own network. Tap into what your friends, clients, and business associates are doing. Where are they networking? Ask if you can tag along. That usually gets the ball rolling. You could also check out mobile apps that help you find people close to you or networking events in your area. Whatever you do, wherever you go, remember ... **MAKE NETWORKING** a **"MARKETING PRIORITY!"**

ReallyFastBooks.com | RichCoachBrokeCoach.com | TVGuest.com

TACTIC #2

IT'S *NOT* WHAT YOU **SAY**,

IT'S WHAT YOU **ASK**!

Questions?

> "You'll get more out of a networking event, and make better use of your time networking if you ask more questions and keep people talking about themselves. Listening puts you in the driver seat of the conversation every time!"
>
> "For true success ask these four questions: What? How? Why? When? and Who? That should get you further along to where you want to go than talking about what you do, first! Try it. See how it works for you too!"
>
> — Bart Smith, TheMarketingMan.com
> & Founder Of TimeToNetwork.com

> "You can have everything in life you want if you will just help enough other people get what they want!"
>
> — Zig Ziglar

BartSmith.com | TimeToNetwork.com | LethalConfidence.com

FINDING OUT WHAT PEOPLE DO & HOW YOU CAN HELP "THEM FIRST" SERVES YOU GREATER THAN YOU TELLING THEM WHAT YOU DO & HOW "YOU NEED HELP, FIRST!"

I know, that was a mouthful, but it's true. What's more, it's normal to feel a little nervous and anxious with a double dose of butterflies in the tummy when you think about attending a networking event. You might ask, "Why so?" Is it because we want to be liked, accepted, and not rejected by total strangers? Probably, among other reasons. Well, not to worry. Wouldn't you like to know the SILVER BULLET to diffuse all those uneasy feelings and learn how to replace them with lethal confidence before heading out to every networking event in your future?

CHANGE YOUR AIM GOING INTO EVERY NETWORKING EVENT FROM "YOU" TO "THEM" ... THAT'S IT!

People attend networking for a lot of reasons. Among those reasons on the list is a "WIIFM" (*What's In It For Me*) thought process. Well, if you think networking is about you and what you can get out of it, just remember this:

DIRECTLY: Assist others first, gladly!

INDIRECTLY: You'll be assisted next, naturally!

You've heard people say, "When I'm rich, I'm going to help everyone I can. In the meantime, I have to survive, so I'll focus mainly on myself and my needs." Well, that will only get you so far. Instead, let's flip it around and watch what happens. I live by this rule ...

> "My focus is to help as many people as I can, within my skills/talents/ideas (i.e., without spreading myself too thin or giving the farm away), in this way, many of the people I help will help me (directly or indirectly) get what I want! *(i.e., ideas, referrals, success, money, happiness, fulfillment, etc.)*

BE OF SERVICE TO OTHERS

Pretty simple. Look at it this way. You'll get to where you want to go much faster if you focus on helping others FIRST. Look at popular artists, musicians, and actors who provide a good time for their fans. How many fans do they bring joy and satisfaction too? A few? A dozen? Hundreds? Thousands? Millions? You get the idea. The more people you help, or the more you do for one person (or a few people) the more they can do for you effortlessly and gladly from the heart! Take this approach into every networking event and watch it work like magic. It's simple math and it works like clockwork. Apply it, work it, and watch it work for you in return. Besides, all the BENEFITS OF NETWORKING I talked about in the last chapter will absolutely come true when you approach networking in this order.

(1) FIRST ... <u>HELP</u> OTHERS

(2) SECOND ... <u>WATCH</u> OTHERS HELP YOU

The reason for this formula is because you'll need to INSPIRE others to help you. Whether they're paid (i.e., referral or affiliate commissions) or they just like you, like what you represent,

TACTIC #2 – IT'S NOT WHAT YOU SAY - IT'S WHAT YOU ASK!

and/or the people you help and in turn want to help you!

HOW CAN YOU BE OF SERVICE TO OTHERS & HELP THEM?

You will never know ... UNTIL YOU ASK!

ASK, "HOW CAN I HELP YOU?"

This is the #1 question to have on your mind when you head out to every networking event. When you walk in the door, the burning question on your mind should be how you can help someone. While you ask people what they do, listen for ways to help them (if you can). This is the ultimate question to ask them before you get to anything remotely talking about yourself.

THE "TOP TEN" WAYS YOU CAN HELP PEOPLE WHO NEED IT

ASK THEM! Oh, I already said that. Really though, people need all kinds of help. Listening to them talk about themselves and their business or passion is the fastest path to you learning how you can help them. YOU then get to decide HOW you can help them:

1. Offer **REFERRALS** (for free/no charge or a commission) ...

2. Offer **RECOMMENDATIONS**, make introductions ...

3. Offer **ENCOURAGEMENT**, support and cheer them on ...

4. Offer **IDEAS**, suggestions, feedback, resources ...

5. Offer to **MENTION THEM** on social media or on your list ...

6. Offer a **JOINT VENTURE** proposal or bundle your products and

services together to form one product/service you both can sell and split the profits. Conduct a seminar/class together!

7. Offer to **INTERVIEW THEM** (or be interviewed) to help promote what it is they do ...

8. **PURCHASE** what they sell because you/someone needs it ...

9. Offer your **PRODUCTS** and/or **SERVICES** to help them ...

10. **HOW** have you **HELPED OTHERS IN THE PAST**? Make note, especially if it worked, and apply it again to others in need.

QUESTIONS, QUESTIONS, QUESTIONS

Naturally, there are other questions to ask before you get to the magical question, *"How can I help you?"* So, let's examine the flow of conversation as it might go when you approach someone to meet at a networking event.

| INITIAL QUESTIONS TO KICK-START VIRTUALLY ANY CONVERSATION | **"Hi, what's your name?"**
"What do you do?"
"Where are you from?"
"How'd you hear about this event?"
"How did you get into your (profession)?
"What are some examples of (what you do or how you do it)?"
"Wow, that's interesting ... tell me more!"
"Is there anything I can do to help you?" |

All these questions keep you in a LEARNING / PROBING MODE

BartSmith.com | TimeToNetwork.com | LethalConfidence.com

while the other person quickly warms up to you inquiring about them, their life, business and/or passion. You know how it goes. What's everyone's favorite subject to talk about? THEMSELVES! Keep the conversation focused on the other person by asking questions probing deeper into what they do to find out specifically if and how you can help them. If you can, then apply one of the **TOP 10 WAYS YOU CAN HELP PEOPLE** you meet at a networking event. Keep asking questions, take mental notes and see where the conversation leads to.

If anything, the other person is going to think you're the greatest for taking your time to listen to their story. How eager do you think they'll be to help you in return? EXACTLY! EAGER? HAPPY? INSPIRED? SMILING ALL THE WAY? You bet!

Suppose though the conversation isn't going well and you want out of that conversation circle? What kind of questions could you ask besides just outright leaving? You might ask questions such as:

> **"Have you met anyone here tonight worth meeting?"**
> **"Would you like to introduce me?"**
> (Maybe he/she will and you can segway easily to the next networking conversation.)
>
> **"Do you know when the event ends? Can we continue this conversation on the phone sometime this week? I'd like to meet some of the other people here tonight before the event ends. Sound good? I look forward to talking again ..."**
> (An honest way to get out of any long-winded conversation every time.)

ReallyFastBooks.com | RichCoachBrokeCoach.com | TVGuest.com

BENEFITS OF ASKING QUESTIONS VS. TALKING ABOUT YOURSELF

Are there any benefits? You bet! You might be talking to someone who is either not your ideal client or doesn't share the same ideology you have about helping others. So, instead, focus your valuable time on them and what their needs are to get to know them better. As you get to know them, try to peel back the layers as to what makes them unique; what they say, how they say it, etc. to give you more insight into the person you are speaking with.

This approach is similar to the response, "No, I don't have any business cards. I prefer to give out my contact information personally and on a need-to-have basis. I just don't go running around handing out business cards for the heck of it."

Likewise, being selective as to who hears your story also comes into play. Better to spend your precious time at the event listening to all those you meet. You might not get that chance again. So, spend your time asking questions and making fewer statements about yourself. If you do talk about yourself, keep it brief and yet use exciting words and phrases that share a little bit about what it is you do.

MORE TIPS FOR CONVERSATION

TALK LESS / LISTEN MORE

It's been our theme for networking conversations so far, hasn't it? Have you heard this saying? "We were born with two ears *and one mouth?"* Translated, it means don't talk *too much* and listen more. Let the other person do most of the talking without interrupting. This will allow you time to think about what's being said so you can reply with information, ideas, and relative questions, which will make a KNOCKOUT FIRST IMPRESSION.

No one likes to be fire hosed with a non-stop spray of never ending words. Talk in sound bites and phrases that can be easily digested mentally. Choose your words wisely. Don't talk over someone's head and remember to pause between thoughts to allow the other person to respond and get a word in edgewise.

Again, keep the focus on the other person. It's perfect to keep the conversations to about 70/30 meaning that 70% represents the time given to the other person to speak and giving you a 30% opportunity to respond and ask more questions to stimulate the conversation and keep it flowing in their (and your) direction.

If you have products/services to sell, focus on outcomes, results, and the experiences of others. Stories sell! So, there's no need to tell folks what you do if you can narrate in an entertaining and effective way. Tell stories about yourself and even better with a sense of humor. Maybe you can relate a success story that would appeal to a group to give them an idea of how you handle certain situations. Just don't overdo it.

DON'T TALK ABOUT YOURSELF WITHOUT BEING ASKED, "WHAT DO YOU DO?"

It's better to wait for a queue to start talking about yourself, rather than jumping into your story with someone who: (1) doesn't care, (2) can't appreciate what you have to say/do, (3) can't use or make a positive referral for you, or (4) _____? It's better to start off any conversation focused on the other person by asking relevant questions and learning what they do best to navigate your way into talking about how you can help them with surgical precision. No one wants to waste time at these events and not everyone will be interested in what you have to say. In most cases it was because they were too much into themselves. Don't let that be you. This should be your cue to politely move on.

DOCUMENT WHAT HE/SHE/YOU SAID "IN THE MOMENT" OR "SHORTLY AFTER!"

In the heat of the moment, whip out your phone and start entering their contact information, send them a text, and/or call them to make a record of your connection. It's hard to remember all the conversations you'll have at networking events especially if it's a large group. So, take a minute (per contact you meet) and make a note or two in a mobile app you might download (i.e., *NoteEverything*) or jot down on the back of their business card handed to you by the people you just spoke to. Jotting down a note or two will help you remember what it was you were going to meet that person about. When you mention those very things in your first eMail correspondence, wow, you're on your way to making a really great FIRST "FOLLOW UP" IMPRESSION!

BartSmith.com | TimeToNetwork.com | LethalConfidence.com

TACTIC #3

BE THE **FIRST** TO FOLLOW UP
&
STAY IN TOUCH ALWAYS!

"Your net worth is in your network, not just in your work."

"Be the first to make contact and you'll be remembered ... not forgotten!"

"Follow up, not just once, but twice and you'll be closer to friend/colleague (status) than stranger for your care in reaching out."

"Networking success is really in the follow up stage, not in the initial first meeting."

"It takes time to network and build your network. It takes seconds to lose it all if you don't follow up."

— Bart Smith, TheMarketingMan.com
& Founder Of TimeToNetwork.com

"FOLLOW UP" IS EVERYTHING!

I like that quote, *"Your net worth is in your network, not just in your work."* So true. Without a customer base, fan base, network of suppliers/vendors and others you can count on to help you maintain a profitable business model, you're almost dead in the water. That's why it's so important to follow up with folks you met at last night's networking event to let them know you're very interested in how you can work together to achieve your mutual goals.

FOLLOW UP FACTS & STATS SAY IT ALL

Have you ever come across these statistics about sales and follow up? They're pretty depressing when you think about it and yet there's room for opportunity. Let's review them:

- 48% of salespeople — **NEVER** follow up with a prospect.
- 25% of salespeople — make one contact and then **STOP**.
- 12% of salespeople — **GIVE UP** after just three contacts.
- ONLY 10% of salespeople — make more than **3 contacts.**
- **2%** of all sales — are made on the 1ST contact.
- **3%** of all sales — are made on the 2ND contact.
- **5%** of all sales — are made on the 3RD contact.
- **10%** of all sales — are made on the 4TH contact.
- **80%** of all sales — are made on the 5TH through 12TH contact.

SOURCE: NATIONAL SALES EXECUTIVE ASSOCIATION

Not that you're in the business of selling to those you network with, but look at those stark figures. We humans are terrible at follow up. What's more, it takes a long time for us to take

ReallyFastBooks.com | RichCoachBrokeCoach.com | TVGuest.com

action on something UNLESS we're contacted A LOT! Not that you have to follow up with new contacts multiple times to get action, but some kind of action is needed ON OUR PART. Doing so, right after the events we attend, will help ensure we don't lose any momentum created with the people we meet at them.

MY "TOP 15" FOLLOW UP TACTICS TO ACT ON SO YOU NEVER LOSE YOUR NETWORKING MOMENTUM

When it comes to following up with people you meet, here are 15 things to keep in mind in order to capitalize on all that time spent networking. Remember, it takes time to build a network. It takes seconds to lose it all if you don't follow up. So, FOLLOW UP!

1. **Create a system (if you don't have one) for organizing leads** you gather from all your networking efforts. It could be as simple as using Excel, Google Contacts, Outlook or some other contact management system.

2. **Google your new contact(s) online** to see what you find. You might discover more information about them that motivates you to follow up with them or NOT. Yikes!

3. **Add their personal/business contact information to your contact system** along with extra information about them. If you found them online after the event from searching, populate their contact profile with as much information as possible including notes about the contact. "Met at XYZ networking event on 00/00/00. Talked about _____."

4. **Out of sight, out of mind**. You know the drill. About 99% of the people you meet will forget about you. Don't you forget

TACTIC #3 — BE THE FIRST TO FOLLOW UP & STAY IN TOUCH

about them. Make plans to contact them within 24-72 hours after each networking event.

5. **If you took pictures, put them up on your website, Facebook, Instagram, and other websites.** Tag them, whenever possible, so their names get associated with your photos. Post them within 24-48 hours to keep the memories of the event fresh and alive!

6. **Follow up on how you promised to help** those you met.

7. **eMail your new contacts** within 24 hours of meeting them. Remind them of who you are, what you talked about and the action/ideas/resources you both discussed upon meeting. You can do this from your phone, most likey. Here's a sample letter:

SUGGESTED SUBJECT:
Bart Smith following up from last night's networking event.

SUGGESTED EMAIL:
Hello _____, I wanted to reach out to say how great it was to meet you. I'm interested in continuing our conversation about ____ when you have time. Let me know what day/time is best for you and we'll pick up the conversation right where we left off. Sound good? Have a great rest of your week.

BART SMITH
(000) 000-0000 CELL/TEXT

Done. See how easy that was? Next!

8. **Call your contacts within 1-3 days** after meeting them.

9. **Contact them on social media**, add them as friends on Facebook and your LinkedIn network, *Like* their Facebook page, Tweet 'em, send them photos you took with them in them for posting, etc.

ReallyFastBooks.com | RichCoachBrokeCoach.com | TVGuest.com

10. **Share your newly formed contacts** with your current friends, associates and colleagues.

11. **Send them something**, perhaps a link to something you want them to check out or that resource you promised to forward. Did you write a book? Send them access to the digital copy online or mail an autographed hard copy after confirming their mailing address.

12. **Blog or write about your networking experience**. What happened? Who did you meet? Share some of the discussions. Communicate it to your blog readers.

13. **Plan to meet in person** for lunch, coffee, etc., to continue your conversation.

14. **Mention other networking events you might be attending** that they might like to know about, and ask them if they know of any you might want to attend.

15. **Call them back after a few weeks or even a couple of months** if you don't hear from them after awhile. You never know. They might have been busy that first week you met, and, now, maybe time has opened up for you to check in. "Bart, I'm so glad you called. I remember speaking with you. Yes, let's get together. How about Wednesday?"

STAY IN TOUCH

The most important aspect of building / maintaining a professional network is **STAYING IN TOUCH**. Maintain those relationships on a regular basis. **REMEMBER, FOLLOW UP SETS YOU APART FROM EVERYONE ELSE.** Lay a foundation to create extraordinary friendships / business relationships essential to **YOUR SUCCESS AND THEIRS!**

BartSmith.com | TimeToNetwork.com | LethalConfidence.com

WRAPPING UP

ENCOURAGING WORDS FROM THE AUTHOR

BART SMITH
TheMarketingMan.com
TimeToNetwork.com

"I no longer think of people as 'strangers.' Instead, we are all related and share similar needs in business and in life. Everyone in this room has a common goal -- to meet someone who can help them with their business ventures, passion, or _____. I am one of those people, just like you. So, all we have to do is talk, listen, and enjoy the experience of networking. Together, we have opportunities to connect and make networking really work! Hello, my name is _____."

— *Bart Smith, TheMarketingMan.com
& Founder Of TimeToNetwork.com*

WRAPPING UP – ENCOURAGING WORDS FROM THE AUTHOR

Networking is more than just marketing, though. It's more than promoting ourselves and what we do and helping others do the same. It's more than what we think networking really is. Networking, underneath it all, after the lights go out at the networking event location you just left, and you go home to reflect on all those you met and the good times you hopefully had ... likely successful networking boils down to:

NETWORKING = PEOPLE HELPING PEOPLE

When you think about networking or attending your next event, consider these points and live up to them with all your energy, might and overflowing, burning enthusiasm to help other people:

- **Make networking a regular activity** in all your marketing efforts. Network somewhere at least once a month!

- **Initiate conversations** with, "Hey, how are you? Tell me about yourself." (ASK, ASK, ASK!)

- **Listen and learn.** Talk less, listen more. Focus on them.

- **No need to hard sell or talk about yourself.** Keep asking questions. The subject of YOU will come up.

- **Take notes, mentally/literally, about your conversations.** Use the back of business cards, your phone, anything. Keep your mind, ears and eyes sharp for inbound ideas that will come out of nowhere! Share them, or keep them to yourself and act on them.

- **Is someone worth a follow up?** Set up your follow up meeting(s) while you're *still* at the event. Contact them within 24-72 hours.

- **Make a lasting impression with people as you go out the door.** "Hey, great meeting you. I'll call you tomorrow."

ReallyFastBooks.com | RichCoachBrokeCoach.com | TVGuest.com

Do these things and you'll leave a lasting impression on all those you meet. Take what you've learned from this book and share it with those you meet online and offline. When you do, not only will you generate more business, leads and potential income, you'll also make new friends and connections that can last a lifetime. Friendships, experiences, good times, and memories. That's what networking has in store for us all!

3 SIMPLE NETWORKING TACTICS

What's more, remember my 3 SIMPLE NETWORKING TACTICS and you'll absolutely succeed at networking wherever you go:

1. Make Networking a "<u>MARKETING PRIORITY</u>!"
2. It's Not What You SAY, It's What You <u>ASK</u>!
3. Be The <u>FIRST</u> To Follow Up & Stay In Touch, <u>ALWAYS</u>!

Remember these very simple networking tactics, and you'll rock at every networking event you attend!

Here's to your "*networking*" success,

Bart Smith

BART SMITH
BartSmith.com
TimeToNetwork.com
RichCoachBrokeCoach.com
CoachingClientForms.com
BartsCookies.com
TVGuest.com
... and more!

BartSmith.com | TimeToNetwork.com | LethalConfidence.com

RESOURCES

MY NETWORKING BOOKS, MY SITES & CHOCOLATE CHIP COOKIES, OF COURSE!

BART'S NETWORKING BOOKS

If you liked *3 SIMPLE NETWORKING TACTICS*, then you'll definitely want to read my other networking books, which can be found at: **BartSmith.com/books**

THIS BOOK STARTED IT ALL! Inside this blueprint on networking are all my personal networking tactics that no other book on networking covers. If you network with others online or offline, this book is a must-have!

INSIDE YOU'LL LEARN:
- How to greet people ...
- What to say to them ...
- How to politely move on when conversations don't meet your needs ...

YOU'LL ALSO GET:
- Opening and exit lines to say ...
- Key questions to ask ...
- How to ask questions ...
- Tips on remembering names ...
- When to arrive /leave and why ...
- How to prepare for an event ...
- What to or not to take ...

You won't find another book on networking written like *My Networking Tactics!* I talk about what your networking goals should be, tools you could use to help you network, your appearance, conversational tactics, actions before/during/after networking events plus how to grow your network beyond the outer limits! Check it out at:

BartSmith.com/books

NO ONE IS EXEMPT from making mistakes when they network. EVEN I MAKE MISTAKES! That's why I wrote this book with a good friend of mine. We saw so many people struggling and hosts making unavoidable mistakes.

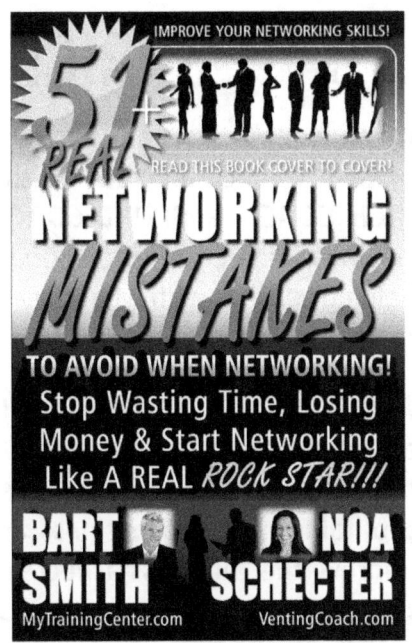

For example, can you relate? "Did I say the right thing?", "Whoops, that didn't come out right ...", or "Oh, I forgot to bring/do/say this ..." That's our point, and that's why we wrote this book.

Inside **51+ NETWORKING MISTAKES**, we go into REGRETTABLE NETWORKING MISTAKES YOU CAN AVOID!

PART I: **BEFORE** NETWORKING
PART II: **WHILE** YOU ARE NETWORKING
PART III: **AFTER** NETWORKING

The cover of the book implies that there are 51+ networking mistakes, but there are so many more! Imagine how much more productive, sharper, you're networking experience could be when you know what some of the networking mistakes are ahead of time! Be prepared to get the most quality out of your conversations and your connections!

For MORE INFORMATION and to get this BOOK and/or the AUDIO VERSION, go to:

BartSmith.com/books

BART'S "RICH COACH BOOK"

If you want to start and operate a successful coaching business, or take your current one to the next level, then you need my **RICH COACH ◆ BROKE COACH** book. For aspiring and current coaches, *Rich Coach Broke Coach* was written with the intent of helping coaches with what they need most in the areas of business, marketing, client interactions, sales, and making money.

RICH COACH ◆ BROKE COACH is your master plan for all that and much more. The manual is rich with nuggets of information that you won't find in other coaching books about how to run a profitable coaching business and offers instructions on how to improve the "business aspect" of your coaching profession.

TOPICS INCLUDE:

Income & Setting Your Fees

Creating Coaching Packages

Contracts & Agreements

Finding Clients

Enrolling Clients

Overcoming Objections

Working With Clients

Coaching Resources

Marketing Tactics

... and much more!

Checking out the coaching forms and this one-of-a-kind coaching manual and order it (in print and/or audio format) at my website:

RichCoachBrokeCoach.com

MY "RICH COACH FORMS"

Every coach (i.e., life, personal and/or business coach) needs their own set of customized coaching/client agreement/assessment forms to help run a successful coaching business. Because many coaches, and those who aspire to be coaches, don't have such forms or know how to create them, I have taken the time to create (and share) the same ones I use with you.

Peruse the following list of coaching forms. It's very complete and the perfect set of forms to launch any coaching business successfully. Each of the forms you see below are for sale separately or as a COMPLETE COACHING & AGREEMENT FORMS BUNDLE, which SAVES YOU OVER $125. Cost? *Just $30 at my website!*

1. Welcome Letter
2. Coaching Client Agreement
3. Client Intake Form
4. Client Self-Assessment Form
5. Free Coaching Gift Certificates
6. Free Coaching Session Agreement
7. Coaching Session Preparation Form
8. Coaching Session Summary Forms
9. Client Call Record (For The Coach)
10. The Wheel Of Life Form
11. Goals & Action Questions
12. Coaching Period Summary Forms
13. Client Feedback/Testimonial Form
14. Coaching / Speaking Hour Log (Excel)

You can learn more about these forms and purchase them separately or as a bundle at my website:

CoachingClientForms.com

BART'S OTHER SELF-HELP BOOKS

If you liked *3 SIMPLE NETWORKING TACTICS*, then you'll definitely want to go to BartSmith.com/books and check out Bart's other books on coaching, personal development, checklists, marketing, social media, and more!

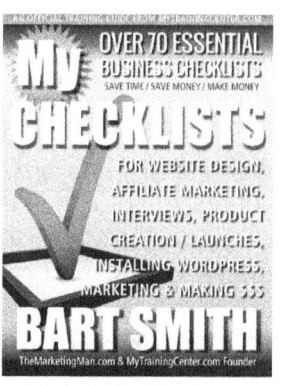

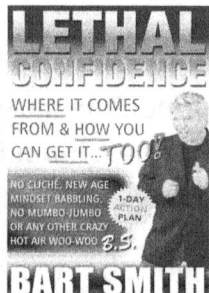

SEE MORE BOOKS, EBOOKS & AUDIO AT:

BartSmith.com/books

BART'S COOKIES

If you really want to know what it's like to be in a heaven-sent, orgasmically addictive, blissfully overloaded state of mind in your relationship with the ONE you love, then you must experience **Bart's world famous chocolate chip cookies**. Besides being an author, Bart commercially bakes dark chocolate chip, milk chocolate chip, white chocolate chip, white chocolate chip with macadamia nuts, peanut butter with milk chocolate chips and his favorite ... a milk+dark chocolate chip combo. Yes, he even bakes gluten-free cookies. All flavors have no preservatives. Check it out along with 350+ cookie reviews by visiting:

BartsCookies.com

"My cookies are always baked fresh and shipped the same day right to your door. To order online, just go to my website."

White Chocolate Chip with Macadamia Nuts

Milk+Dark Chocolate Chip "Combo" Cookie (Guaranteed Always To Blow Your Mind!)

www.ingramcontent.com/pod-product-compliance
Lightning Source LLC
Chambersburg PA
CBHW061228180526
45170CB00003B/1212